Get Found, Get Liked, Get Patients

Making the Most of Social Media

Rita Zamora

Get Found, Get Liked, Get Patients

Printed by: CreateSpace Independent
Publishing Platform

Copyright © 2018, Rita Zamora

Published in the United States of America

170622-00843-3

ISBN-13: 978-1726152952
ISBN-10: 1726152952

For more information on 90-Minute Books including finding out how you
can publish your own book, visit 90minutebooks.com or call (863) 318-0464

Here's What's Inside...

Foreword

There are many social media "experts" out there these days. It seems practically anyone who has had a Facebook page for more than a year is ready to dispense advice and charge for it. Rita Zamora is a different story. I've known Rita for almost 8 years, and I consider her one of the very few people in the dental industry who actually is an expert in the field. Rita is more than just an extremely accurate guide through the twisted maze of social media; she also gives realistic expectations to her clients. In a world of hype and misinformation, this makes her even more valuable, in my mind. There is no faster moving target in practice marketing than social media. It changes almost daily. Rita is exactly the guide we need. She is both thoughtful and experienced, and this book is her gift of truth and wisdom. Enjoy it, learn from it, and apply it, and your practice will thrive.

— Fred Joyal
Founder, 1-800-DENTIST
Author of *Everything is Marketing and Becoming Remarkable*

Introduction

Get Found, Get Liked, Get Patients - Making the Most of Social Media

Like many of you reading this book, I am a dental person. I became part of a "dental family" after I joined a small, three-person periodontal team more than 20 years ago. Over the course of 15 years, I helped the periodontist who owned the practice grow it to five periodontists and more than 20 team members. I grew to love the profession of dentistry and learned a lot about business development for general and specialty practices.

I am grateful to the periodontist with whom I worked for many years: Dr. Marc Reissner. He was an exceptional practice owner, business leader, and mentor. He encouraged my education and professional growth, and flexed my work schedule to accommodate my college class schedule. While working full-time, I completed a Bachelor's degree with an emphasis in business and marketing and proudly graduated Magna Cum Laude from the University of Colorado. I thought I might leave dentistry to enter the business world and further my career after graduation, but instead, I decided it was the combination of business AND dentistry that I truly loved.

When I worked in the practice, I most enjoyed growing relationships with patients and referral partners. Those relationship aspects of dentistry brought me to where I am today. I feel a special loyalty for dental professionals, and to this day, I feel as if I'm working in each and every one of our clients' practices. We are committed to work that's always in the best interest of the dentist or specialist and their practice.

Enjoy the book! I hope it informs and motivates you to leverage social media to get found, get liked, and get patients. :)

To Your Success!

Rita Zamora

Why Some Dentists Don't Leverage Social Media to Get New Patients

There are several common reasons dentists aren't already using social media to get new patients in the doors. You might think it has to do with a dentist's age - whether or not they were born in the era of social media, but that's not always the case. I've spoken with Millennial dentists, and even dental students, who love social media from a personal standpoint and may even be very active on Instagram or Snapchat, but don't know how to market or promote themselves on Facebook, where patients aged 35 and up spend their time. Dentists of all ages know mature patients are prime candidates for dental implants, sleep dentistry, clear braces, and smile makeovers. Facebook is a major platform for these patients.

It's interesting - after years of trying to convince mature dentists of social media's value, there are now young dentists and dental students questioning whether they too need to stretch their social media comfort zone in order to reach a variety of patients.

Another reason dentists might not use social media to promote their practice is because of time. Maybe your team is busy and has no time to manage social media. You might picture this scenario: patients in the office being ignored while team members stare at their phones to "play with Facebook or Instagram."

Or you may want to leverage social media but aren't sure how to get started. You don't know which tools to use, what to post, or how often to post. Envisioning all the work involved in understanding "social media stuff" is enough to turn you off.

I hear from some dentists that they don't use or like social media because the thought of using a tool with which they are unfamiliar is both intimidating and frustrating. Even dentists who enjoy social media personally may feel overwhelmed by the planning, posting, and campaign management involved in social media marketing. I hope to show you how to bring social media into your practice, so it isn't seen as a "waste of time," but results in new patients via expanded visibility and word of mouth.

The truth is, patients expect to access information about everything 24 hours a day, 7 days a week. Smartphone ownership rose from just 35% of U.S. adults in 2011 to 77% in 2018, according to a Pew Research Center survey on smartphone ownership.[1] With most of your patients able to research anything anytime, it's more important than ever for your practice to have an extensive online presence. Patients are doing tremendous amounts of research before they make that first appointment with a practice or accept big treatment plans a dentist proposes.

Patients aren't just looking for your contact information, either. They expect to know more than they ever have before. They want to know exactly what they can expect at their first appointment, what you look like, what you sound like, what your team is like, how you're involved in the community, and so on.

What the Research Shows

A few key pieces of research help to substantiate why social media and an abundance of online information are important.

Google commissioned a study to learn about the process most people go through when they're looking for new products and services. The research showed that even when people do some online research and come across your website, they continue on a path of research beyond that.[2]

That's important for practice owners to understand because they often think patients will find their websites and become their patients. It's not that straightforward. Research shows that after patients find your website, they'll often want to read reviews, see some social proof, and find out if others are saying you're as awesome as your website says you are.

If you have videos available on a YouTube channel or on your Facebook page or website, patients want to watch those. They may check with their social network, asking their Facebook friends if they've ever heard of you, or they might ask their neighbors in a Facebook group which dentists or specialists they recommend. Only after going through this process do people feel comfortable enough to make an appointment to become a new patient.

A different study commissioned by Facebook shows that even though people tend to think smartphones make it much easier for people to make purchase decisions, many don't realize buyer behavior continues to evolve.

In fact, research shows people are looking for more information than ever before. Think back to the days when people used travel agents to book trips. Those people had one touchpoint. The travel agent consulted with a client, made recommendations for vacations, and booked the hotel, the flight, everything.

Today, it's easy to research and book a trip online yourself, but data from Facebook shows that people planning a trip visit an average of 56 travel-related digital touchpoints.[3] If people require 56 touchpoints just to book a vacation, imagine how many touchpoints are involved in finding a new healthcare provider, dentist, or specialist. This is very important research to consider.

Does your practice have the online presence to support all the digital touchpoints patients require today?

There's also research specific to healthcare. Like Google's consumer study, a study was conducted on behalf of CareCredit™ called The Path to Purchase.[4] The study, an online survey of nearly 2,000 consumers, revealed not only the path people typically follow to become new patients, but also to accept treatment and pay for it. It's one thing to be able to attract new patients with marketing; it's another altogether to convert the patient and have them pay for treatment. CareCredit's Path to Purchase study essentially shows that **three of the five steps it takes to attract a new patient and have them accept and pay for treatment involve extensive research by the patient.** The study revealed, "An average of 76 days is spent on research across the six healthcare categories studied – dentistry, ophthalmology, optometric care, veterinary care, cosmetic procedures and hearing health; with cosmetic procedures taking the longest amount of time - at nearly 145 days."[5]

Where do people do research on dentists and specialists today? They do it primarily online or through word of mouth. The commonality among these studies is that consumers/patients do a tremendous amount of research. They research their practitioner options. They research your practice and what other people say about you. They research the treatment options you recommend. They research options about finances. They may also share and discuss their findings with their friends, family, or social network.

This shows why it's so important for your practice to have an abundance of online information. That doesn't just mean having a good website. You need information in the places where patients spend their time: Facebook, Google Reviews, Instagram, and other social media platforms and online review sites, depending on your practice and what kind of patient you're trying to attract.

An added benefit to having an active presence on social media is the opportunity to be discovered by patients who may not be searching for a dentist, but who run across you coincidentally. Think "discovery" economy vs. "search" economy. The discovery economy is disrupting, shifting, and propelling new business, such as ColourPop, a 2014 online cosmetic company who has become known as a major player in the makeup industry. Compare them to Revlon, a brick and mortar business that's been around since 1932. ColourPop has made Instagram its primary focus and sales funnel and amassed over 5 million Instagram followers, approximately four times as many as the well-established Revlon.[6]

You may be thinking, "Followers are great, but how does that translate to actual business or value?" Coty, another well-established global beauty company, in the ranks of Revlon, announced in February 2018 that "it was rebranding its CoverGirl, Clairol and Max Factor products, to attract younger spenders and compete with affordable and Instagram-popular brands like NYX, Winky Lux and ColourPop."[7] In addition, Kylie Cosmetics and ColourPop, who share manufacturing facilities and management, are also at the top of Deloitte's 2017 list of independent brands to watch.[8] Social media savvy propelled ColourPop to go from a dark horse to an industry leader.

Is your practice positioned to be easily discovered?

With So Many Challenges to Using Social Media, Is It Worth the Trouble?

Imagine you've just moved into a new area of town, and you need to find a new dentist. A couple of friends recommend two different dentists to you: Dr. A and Dr. B. You decide to do some online research to get to know a bit more about Dr. A and Dr. B before you make a decision about the best dentist for you and your family.

First, you check out Dr. A's website and find that he's located in a convenient part of town and he has an impressive CV. His educational background and clinical skills are excellent, so you decide to look a bit further into Dr. A to get to know more about who he is. You soon discover there's only one photo of Dr. A on his website, and it's a professional photo. He's wearing a suit and tie and has a friendly smile. There's not a whole lot more to tell about Dr. A just based on that one photo.

When you research Dr. B, you find he has a similar professional photo of himself on his website, a stellar CV, and great clinical skills. Dr. B also has a Facebook page and Instagram account. On his social media you see pictures showing him running a marathon, spending time outdoors with his wife and two children, fly fishing in the mountains in a beautiful stream, and cycling with his family. There's also a picture of Dr. B's two dogs, a chocolate lab and a yellow lab. You see Dr. B in a number of settings, allowing you to see both his professional and human side.

When I teach live seminars, I go through this exercise with the audience and have them shout out their opinions and perspectives on Dr. A and Dr. B. When it comes to Dr. A, it's interesting to see how people respond. They often furrow their eyebrows and look at me like I'm asking a trick question. They don't understand how they could get to know Dr. A based on one photo.

They start to make things up about Dr. A. They say he looks young, he looks old, he looks friendly, he looks grumpy, he looks like he's not a very happy dentist. They continue to imagine things about Dr. A because that's what people tend to do when they're trying to get to know someone and only have one photo to base their opinions on. It's difficult to get to know someone from just one professional photo.

When I show pictures of Dr. B during a live program, I see the body language and energy of the room shift. It's palpable. People smile, and their body language changes from crossed arms when looking at Dr. B's single professional photo to leaning forward when they see Dr. B in a variety of settings. Within seconds I witness people starting to grow trust in Dr. B before they've even met him in person.

When I ask audience members what their feelings are about Dr. B, they tend to say, "He seems like a nice guy. He seems like someone I would like to get to know." They also label him as a family man and someone who loves dogs. They often share their opinions with smiles on their faces. They say, "He enjoys being outdoors, and he loves nature. So do I and that makes me feel like we have some sort of connection."

Social media is beneficial for dentists and specialists because the more information people can see about who someone is as a person, their human side, the more they can build trust with that individual. That allows a new patient coming into your practice to feel like they already have a relationship with you. When there's an element of trust, the patient is more likely to:

- Accept your big treatment plans and recommendations

- Remain loyal to your practice

- Refer friends and family to your practice

- Leave positive reviews of your practice.

    That, in turn, equates to more new patients and a thriving practice based on social media activities and pictures. How awesome is that?

We'd like to see every dentist leverage social media in such a way that they start to build trust with patients before the patients even

meet them... And make it easy for patients to find and like them. That's the goal.

The Benefits of Social Media

In addition to attracting new patients, there are many different ways to be successful with social media. By "successful," I mean, how will you benefit from social media marketing? Some people immediately think you can only measure benefit in new patients. Sure, that's one way to think of the value. However, there are many other valuable benefits to using social media to promote and grow your practice—including:

Online Reputation & Social Proof

Social media offers practices a strong online reputation thanks to the reviews and positive comments people are able to share on Facebook or review sites. As the studies mentioned earlier indicate,

Social proof is a key requirement for patients vetting potential dental providers. People today want to see that you really are as wonderful as your website claims you are.

Specific to healthcare, a study published in the Journal of the American Medical Association showed more than 60% of patients consult reviews before selecting providers.[9] (If your practice is short on reviews and testimonials, read on for tips to grow them.)

Social-savvy patients know they can often click on individual reviews and testimonials to learn more about who is leaving the reviews. Practices who have legitimate, glowing reviews allow patients to see what they may have in common with other patients—which is what your practice should strive for. **Like attracts like.** When your ideal patients can easily see other patients they share things in common with, this helps to support the decision for them to choose you as their dental home.

Most importantly, having a variety of online reviews helps protect your practice in the event of a poor review. There is no better way to minimize a negative review than to drown it in a sea of positive comments about your practice.

Visibility

Social media can easily help your practice expand visibility beyond the borders of your brick and mortar location. Not only can you connect with patients within the ZIP codes of your choice, you can also reach friends of your existing patients. In marketing terms, when people who don't know you discover your connection to friends, this provides social proof. Facebook or Instagram users can often see if their friends have liked or followed you. This type of marketing outreach is exponentially more beneficial than reaching out "cold" to people who've never heard of you and have no connection to you or your practice. So, in addition to visibility within the ZIP codes of your choice, you have the added benefit of social proof, where potential patients can see their friends giving you a virtual endorsement in the form of likes, follows, or reviews. Other than word of mouth in person-to-person conversations, this type of social proof is unique to social media—how awesome is that?

Trust and Relationships

As I illustrated in the example of Dr. A and Dr. B, social media allows you to begin to establish trust with patients within a matter of seconds. It may only take one photo for you to attract and connect with a potential new patient. Social media also allows you to develop relationships with patients who already know you. Many people and practices are so busy today that there is often little time to stop and chitchat about what's new in your lives. Social media helps to fill that relationship-building gap. Whether you share your love of dogs, your passion for cycling, or the Missions of Mercy projects you volunteer for, <u>social media allows you to share the human side of your practice—this is invaluable</u>.

Trust is the foundation of any healthy relationship, and the doctor-patient relationship is no different. The trust factor has been linked to patients' acceptance of treatment, their satisfaction with recommendations and care, and more. Will you leverage the power of social media to share your human side, make connections with patients, and grow relationships and trust for your practice?

Highlight Services or Be Known as An Authority

If you are already active on social media, what does your social media say about you and your practice? In addition to letting patients see your human side, there should also be content or posts about the type of dentistry or specialty treatments you want to do more of. Some practices have become so good at sharing their human side that they forget we also need to let patients know what type of dentistry you prefer to offer!

For example, if you offer full-service dental implant care, sleep apnea treatments, clear braces, smile makeovers, wisdom tooth extractions, or any other treatments you'd like to be doing more of or become known for, you need to share about those topics on your social media. Take a look at your social media today and see if patients scrolling through your pages will see those treatments highlighted. Yes, social media should be social; however, you also need to be strategic in order to fully leverage—and benefit from—social media for your practice.

A Special Note for Specialists

I spoke with a specialist recently who told me social media didn't really apply to him. The specialist said that long-term patient relationships "aren't a priority like they are for general dentists who see the same patient year after year." Interesting, I thought. If you do one root canal, remove a pair of wisdom teeth, or provide dental implant care for a patient, who's to say that their friends, family, neighbors, or colleagues won't also need similar care from you?

Also keep in mind, patients of specialists are doing their own online research—even if they are referred. I remember back in my treatment coordinator days, patients would walk into the perio practice I worked at with several business cards in hand and say, "My dentist referred me to you, but she also gave me a few other periodontist's business cards and told me any of these options would be great." Referred patients are checking out all their options online as well. And while they are coming with a vote of confidence from their dentist, patients know they can find details online and make informed decisions they can feel confident about. For specialists who are marketing direct to consumer, social media becomes even more important from both a reputation and visibility standpoint.

Does Social Media Really Work for Attracting New Patients?

"Hello. Do you happen to have any appointments available for a first-time patient either today or tomorrow? Thank you!"

This is a Facebook message from a new patient asking to schedule an appointment—yes, via Facebook. As the managers of social media accounts for many dental practices across the country, we get to see firsthand how often people inquire about becoming patients. We even see people ask questions such as, "Are your phones down? I've been trying to reach your office for the past two days and no one answers."… "Do you accept my insurance?" … "My crown just fell off, what should I do?"

Social media is a place where patients are already spending their time. Yes, it can work to attract and help convert new patients, but I hope you'll also consider how beneficial social media is as a convenient communication tool.

The next example is of a father-daughter practice where both father and daughter were hesitant about using social media. When I spoke to the father dentist, he said, "I'm getting ready to retire and sell my practice to my daughter. I don't want to get involved in social media."

The daughter was fresh out of dental school and said, "I'm not ready to get back into social media.

I'm not excited about running into my college friends on Facebook or Instagram."

Despite their hesitations, they opened up to the idea of social media as they felt their city was progressive and they "had no choice." Neither one of them was excited about getting involved with social media until a patient came into their practice shortly after we created their Facebook page and Instagram account and said, "I specifically became a patient because of some of the photos I saw on your Facebook page." The patient liked the idea of a father-daughter dental practice. After seeing the impact a few photos could have on a new patient, both father and daughter were sold and open to new methods of social media marketing.

There are countless stories like this. Even Millennial dentists who are active on Instagram or Snapchat and love social media, see challenges in sometimes having to get to know different aspects of social media to cater to the Baby Boomers they want to attract. A young dentist who recently attended one of my seminars told me he sees several new patients a month from their Instagram and Snapchat efforts. He said, "It's hard for some dentists who don't embrace social media to imagine these benefits because they don't understand what's happening on a platform they don't use." Whether it's the social proof they provide, the photographs they share, or the different ads they run, dentists *are* connecting with and attracting new patients from social media.

As I mentioned earlier, specialists are sometimes skeptical and feel like social media isn't important for them, but not all specialists feel that way. Consider a specialist with a new practice who grew to multiple locations within a few short years because he differentiated himself from other specialists in the state who were ignoring social media. He leveraged various social media tools to get the word out about his practice to referring dentists, as well as to consumers in the area. Social media and being a hip, progressive specialist became a part of their practice brand and created awesome success for them.

Later in the book we will discuss tracking and various tools available to determine where patients are finding or seeing you online.

What if we haven't started yet? Is it too late?

It's not too late. Because social media is so dynamic, there is always a need to shift strategies. For you, it will mean you can launch with whatever the best current strategy is. You're in the right place.

Let me tell you about a dentist who sat in the front row of one of my seminars. She was a mom to two young children, a dentist, and an entrepreneur who owned her own practice. She was feeling overwhelmed and nervous about what social media would mean for her practice. She interpreted it as being a lot of work and stress over things she didn't know a lot about.

Fortunately, my program motivated her! She told me that after the seminar, she shot into action. Based on several tips I gave her at the seminar, she created her brand-new Facebook Business page. She took updated photos of her team and motivated them to invite their local friends and family to like the practice's business page as well. Her team also role played how to invite their patients to share their testimonials and reviews, and once they felt clear on how to have these conversations with patients, they sprung into action.

Over the course of two weeks, she grew a tremendous amount of social proof for her practice. She went from having nothing but a website to having a Facebook page with more than 250 page likes. They received over 15 patient reviews, and countless interactions and positive comments about her and her team because of their updated photos.

Getting started and establishing social proof doesn't have to take a lot of time, and it doesn't have to be stressful or frustrating. This dentist is a great example of how putting a plan in place, getting the motivation needed to implement it, and enlisting the team can result in crucial social proof and valuable benefits for the practice. Most importantly, by becoming easily visible, this dentist also removed a barrier to new patients: being anonymous online.

There are countless dentists and specialists who are easily discovered on social media, growing strong online reputations and social proof every day, and continuing to establish and grow relationships and trust with patients. **Will you be one of them?**

Getting Found

It used to be that having an awesome website which performed well on Google was all you needed to get found online, but times have changed. Today, you need what I like to call "multiple pieces of online real estate." This includes having a robust presence on all the social media platforms your ideal patient spends time on. That could include Facebook, Instagram, LinkedIn, or YouTube... It definitely includes online review sites like Google reviews, Yelp, or Healthgrades™.

So, how do dentists get found by patients on social media? There are two primary methods; the first is through patient research. Think back to the studies mentioned earlier in the book that support patients doing a substantial amount of research while vetting practices. During this research process, patients may search for online reviews, or perhaps they just want to see if you have photos, videos, or information that your website does not include.

The other method that gets your practice found on social media is through unexpected discovery. Every day, people who use social media are spontaneously discovering people, products, and services. In this case, a patient may not intend to find a new dentist, but they happen across your name or your practice by way of a local hashtag, mention in a neighborhood group, or check-ins/tags from friends (social media check-ins and tags create links to your practice that patients can click on to learn more about you).

For those of you unsure what a hashtag is or how it works, know that a hashtag is a word or multi-word phrase with the # symbol directly in front of it. Hashtags allow people to organize content and track discussion topics, and they are also searchable. On Instagram, you can also follow hashtag topics.

For example, here are a few location-specific hashtags:

#Denver

#OrangeCounty

#NYC

An excellent method for your practice to be discovered is through use of your local city or neighborhood hashtags. If you are on Instagram, you should absolutely be taking advantage of the visibility they offer by using local hashtags, specific to your practice location, on a consistent basis.

Which social media platforms matter?

The answer to that question lies in who the patient is you're trying to attract to your practice. Different patients spend time on different platforms. According to Pew Research Center's 2018 Social Media Fact Sheet[10], Facebook is the most widely-used of the major social media platforms. However, ask some teenagers or Millennials which platform they prefer and you may hear them say they don't use the F-word (Facebook) and they prefer Instagram or Snapchat. Let's consider the data to help determine where the different types of patients spend their time. Here's what the 2018 Pew Research Social Media Fact Sheet showed:

Percentage of US adults who use at least one social media site, by age:

88% of 18-29 year olds

78% of 30-49 year olds

64% of 50-64 year olds

37% of 65+ year olds

Percentage of US adults who use each social media platform as of January 2018:

68% Facebook

35% Instagram

29% Pinterest

27% Snapchat*

25% LinkedIn

24% Twitter

73% YouTube

* Snapchat's largest user base is teenagers and young adults, ages 18-29.

Ask anyone which social media platform is most popular and relevant, and they are likely to say whichever their favorite platform is. It's easy to let personal bias guide our business decisions, which is why it's important to consider the data as well as the preferences of your specific patients. Keep in mind we will likely have an entirely different discussion in the years to come, as teens and young adults age. Time will tell which platforms the teens and tweens of today (patients in the years to come) will prefer in the future. For now, in this book, it's Millennials, Generation X, and Baby Boomers we will focus on reaching (see age categories for each below). For practices catering to teens and tweens, you may need to explore Snapchat if you aren't already, and that is an entirely different topic for another book.

Baby Boomers - Born approximately 1946-1964

Generation X - Born approximately 1965-1980

Millennials - Born approximately 1981-1997

Facebook

Let's start with getting found on Facebook. There are several key strategies and tactics you can implement with Facebook that will help grow your visibility, increase your likes, and help you get found.

Facebook Wi-Fi

Facebook Wi-Fi is free of charge. Once set up, the option prompts a Wi-Fi alert to appear in patients' Facebook apps on their smartphones while they're in your practice, asking if they would like to check in on Facebook. If you're not familiar with the Facebook app and checking in at locations, know it's a great opportunity for you to increase word-of-mouth about your practice. For those patients not interested in checking in on Facebook, they can click on an option to simply use your Wi-Fi instead. Create printed signs to place around the practice so patients can easily see that you offer Wi-Fi.

What I love most about Facebook Wi-Fi is that it's _free_ and _automated_. When talking about marketing, those are two words we love to hear!

Other organic, essential tactics you can use to grow your visibility on Facebook are:

- Invite your team to actively like and share your posts

- Invite team members to tag themselves in photos

- Invite team members to brainstorm and help generate ideas for contests and other fun campaigns

The synergy of your team can greatly increase your practice social media visibility. It can also be a form of team-building when you allow willing team members to participate and be involved.

Boosts, Sponsored Posts, and Ads

The other tool you must use if you want to grow your visibility on Facebook is Facebook ads. Facebook has become a pay-to-play tool, so unless you have some unique unicorn presence on the platform, you have to pay to get in front of people's eyes because the marketplace has gotten crowded.

For those of you opposed to ads of any kind, let me elaborate before you skip over this important recommendation. Some doctors are under the impression that any kind of advertising will involve discounting your services or force you to offer "specials" to lure patients in the door. That's not the type of ads I'm suggesting. Facebook offers a number of paid options, which you may hear referred to as boosted posts, sponsored posts, ads, promotions, or direct advertisements. There are a multitude of excellent advertising options available, which allow you to:

- Expand your visibility among patients who know you and have liked your page

- Expand your visibility to the friends of patients who have liked your page

- Expand your visibility to people who aren't connected to your page or practice in any way yet

You are also able to target your ads in many ways, including:

- Age, gender
- Location: City, state, or ZIP code
- Interests: Homeowners, fitness and wellness, or parenting, for example.
- Retargeting: Using a tracking pixel (code installed on your website) to target people who have visited your website
- Custom Audiences: Email addresses that you upload to use for targeting (check with your risk management advisor as to HIPAA guidelines)

Years ago when Facebook pages were relatively new, it was easier for your practice to be visible on Facebook. Fast forward to recent years, when over 1,500 stories compete for a spot in an individual's Facebook News Feed at any given time, yet only about 300 of those stories are chosen to appear. Those stats were shared by Facebook in 2014[11], meaning its likely even higher competition today. In addition, the News Feed ranks each possible story (from more to less important) by looking at thousands of factors relative to each person. All of this has led to major decreases in visibility—unless you leverage Facebook ads.

Note that you do not have to have a large budget to be effective with Facebook ads. It's reasonable to start with a modest budget of $50 per month, for example. Yes, there are practices spending in the hundreds or thousands of dollars per month, but they tend to be the exception. If you have been in practice for many years, you may recall having to pay just to have your phone number listed in the white pages—how crazy was that? Paying for visibility on Facebook is nothing more than a shift in your marketing budget (and your mindset) from old-school to modern strategies.

Want to know, step by step, how to best boost your Facebook posts? Check out and download my latest 5 X 5 Boost Formula at **www.RitaZamora.com/SpecialBookBonus**.

Virtual Door-Knocking and Handshaking

Another great strategy to expand your visibility on Facebook (and Instagram too) is business-to-business networking. Think of this as virtual door-knocking and handshaking... Like and follow other business pages—from your practice page—so the likes and comments appear on behalf of your practice. When others see your likes, comments, and hellos coming from your page, they often will reciprocate and like you back.

Make a list of businesses or organizations you support that you could possibly network with. This might include those who serve similar demographics to your patients or potential referral sources in the community:

- Hospitals

- Schools

- Restaurants you enjoy

- Patients who are realtors, artists, authors, or public figures

- Organizations, groups, or non-profits - for example, Veterans groups, Girl Scouts, Habitat for Humanity, or the local humane society.

The cost of this networking is your time, effort, and energy. You can generate some good will in your community and it will help you get found, too.

Of course, there are many other Facebook strategies and tactics you can also use, and more will be mentioned further in this book. However, note that new options are rolling out, and changing, almost daily. Sign up for Rita's email updates or follow Rita Zamora Connections on social media for more timely tips: RitaZamora.com.

If you are not yet set up on Facebook, you can get started and learn more at facebook.com. You will need a Personal Profile (individual's account) for you or a team member to administer/manage your account and a Business Page for your practice.

Instagram

Another important social media tool that will help you get found is Facebook-owned Instagram. Some people might say Instagram is THE most important tool—in their opinion. It's not unusual for some practices to put all their social media resources into Instagram, which makes sense if all of your ideal patients are only on Instagram, right? Instagram's popularity has skyrocketed in the last few years. In 2017, CNBC reported that Instagram added 100 million new users in just four months, it's fastest-ever growth rate. That same year, Instagram added the Stories feature to their platform. Stories allow users to post photos and videos that disappear within 24 hours—similar to Snapchat's beloved feature. For comparison, 200 million people used Instagram Stories in 2017, compared to Snapchat's 161 million.[12]

Instagram is a visual economy. Words won't get noticed unless you have a great visual to capture someone's attention. Statisticbrain.com said the average human attention span is 8.25 seconds, less than that of a goldfish at 9 seconds.[13] If you want to get found and noticed, you've got to share something appealing to look at. Appealing can be defined differently by everyone. (More on that later in the Perfection Paralysis section.)

Photos and video are what it's all about—there are no reviews, no services tabs, and you are currently limited to one website link in your

Instagram bio. If you want to get found and noticed on Instagram, you need to think photos and video. People want to see images that are attractive, beautiful, or unique. If you want patients to follow you on both Facebook and Instagram, remember to mix up your content so you aren't taking up News Feed space with duplicate content. Again, your main focus on Instagram should be visual.

If you love taking photos, congratulations: Instagram content generation will be easy for you. In some cases, practices might decide to hire a photographer to visit their practice and snap a variety of photos and video to share in the future. Use any of the multitudes of apps available and you can make almost any image look fabulous with cropping, lighting, filters, etc., or for brands that support fun, add text, doodles, or stickers to your images or videos.

For those of you unfamiliar with Instagram, it's free to open an account. Note that while you can view Instagram accounts from a desktop browser, your options are currently limited. To easily use all the bells and whistles of Instagram offers, you will need to use the tool from an app on a smartphone or tablet.

Here are a few steps to get started:

1) Download the Instagram app on the mobile device of your choice—it's free!

2) Set up your profile. You can set your profile to private if you want to explore incognito.

3) Follow businesses, people, or perhaps get inspired by what other dental practices are doing.

Once your practice is set up on Instagram, there are a variety of tactics you can use to help expand your visibility, grow followers, and attract patients. Here are a few tips:

Invite Patients to Join You

- You can let your patients know your practice is on Instagram (and other social media) in a variety of ways:

- Invite Facebook followers to join you on Instagram

- Include the Instagram logo and link on your practice website and other online profiles

- Print the Instagram logo on reception signage, business cards, and other marketing materials

- Announce your Instagram presence in your patient e-newsletters

- Offer patients a goodie like a personalized lip balm (or, depending on your local regulations, an entry for a contest) when they check-in or tag your practice on Instagram

Network Business-to-Business

Like Facebook, Instagram is a great place to network business-to-business. You can follow local businesses, like the posts they share, and comment on their activities. To your patients or other business owners, these actions would show up as a message (notification) like, "Dr. Smith's Dental Practice liked or commented on so-and-so's Instagram post." Again, this virtual door-knocking and handshaking is extremely effective in getting the word out about your practice and helping you to get found.

Include Location Hashtags

Remember to frequently use your location hashtags in Instagram posts and Stories. Stories is a feature that lets users post photos and videos that vanish after 24 hours. While there currently isn't data available to support people specifically searching for a new dentist on Instagram, it makes sense to use hashtags or stickers that refer to your practice location. In the event that someone does search "[Your City] Dentist" on Instagram, you want to make sure your practice shows up. Try it for yourself.

While using the Instagram app:
- Enter your town and "dentist" in the Instagram search, e.g., "Denver Dentist", and see what pops up.

- Enter your local or neighborhood hashtag, e.g., #Denver, in the search and explore—this is where you want to be sure your practice shows up for your area.

Leverage Sponsored Posts or Ads

Like Facebook, Instagram offers options to pay for sponsored posts or ads that will help your practice expand visibility within specific ZIP codes and among the demographic(s) of your choice. In fact, Facebook offers an option where your Facebook ads can automatically populate to Instagram as well, but you can also place ads specifically for Instagram. You can explore opportunities for as little as a few dollars per day.

Since we are still focused on getting found, I also recommend you create a profile on other social media platforms as well. Listed below are platforms on which you'll want to set up a profile or page for your practice. Whether or not you're going to actively use a social media platform, it's beneficial to set up your account, add your practice website link, and enhance the *About* section with some interesting and engaging information about your practice. You may even want to add a few posts, with key photos or video to show off. I'll explain why you may or may not need to do anything beyond the basic setup I just described.

Here are the different platforms we'll review:

- Twitter
- LinkedIn
- Pinterest
- Snapchat
- YouTube

Twitter is a tool we've helped many practices and other businesses leverage for years. It may or may not be effective for your practice. If it has been helpful in getting your practice found, that is wonderful. For the majority of practices, I recommend setting up your profile and either auto-posting from your Facebook or Instagram account to your Twitter account or simply populating the account with your practice website link and contact information. Unless you have someone in your practice with a special affinity for Twitter, chances are Twitter will not be worth spending marketing resources on— spend your time and money more predictably, elsewhere.

LinkedIn is another piece of online real estate where you might be found. Known as the business suit of social media, you can set up both individual and business accounts. Business pages are called Company Pages on LinkedIn. You can set up a Company Page for your practice and individual accounts for the doctors in your practice. However, the amount of time, effort, and energy I recommend you spend beyond that will vary depending on your practice type.

If you're a specialist, LinkedIn could be a great tool for connecting and networking with local referring doctors and/or hospitals, etc. Think business-to-business networking. You may also want to explore LinkedIn paid ads for your Company Page to promote educational events you are hosting or to promote your speciality services. If you are a general dentist, you may simply find a lot of salespeople trying to connect with you via your individual LinkedIn profile. Everyone is different. If you have a special love for LinkedIn, there are surely networking opportunities for you there.

Pinterest is another piece of online real estate. Depending on the type of practice you have, it may or may not be worth your time. For the majority of practices, I recommend just setting up a profile and populating it with your practice info. Unless you have one of those unicorn-type practices that does something amazing with their Pinterest, you're probably not going to get the same benefit you would from Instagram or Facebook. Yes, there are practices out there that are active on Pinterest. If you see success from your Pinterest efforts, kudos! For the majority of practices, though, Pinterest is best left to the fashionistas and interior decorators.

Snapchat - Do you need to snap? This platform is not limited to tweens, teens, and young adults; however, they form the majority of its user base. You can find dentists and specialists actively using Snapchat as a marketing/visibility tool today, but this tool is not recommended for every practice.

When using any of these tools, you always have to consider your resources and where your interests lie. For example, I had a dentist approach me who told me she loved Instagram and wasn't really into Facebook. She wanted to manage her own social media presence. It made sense for this dentist to delegate her Facebook management to a team member or outside vendor but to handle her Instagram marketing herself—because that is what she wanted to do. This worked perfectly because she was passionate and excited about Instagram, and she already had a huge following there.

The same goes for Snapchat. I've spoken with several dentists who have said, "We're very active on Snapchat because that's what we love to use! We've gotten patients from our use of Snapchat." In those cases, I recommend that willing Snapchat-loving dentists manage their own Snapchat efforts because that is where their interests lie. For a practice where there is zero interest in Snapchat and their patients are mainly on Instagram and Facebook, it makes no sense to spend resources, time, effort, energy, or money on Snapchat.

YouTube is a valuable place for your practice to be found. I'm often asked if you should have a YouTube channel for your practice and the answer is <u>yes</u>. A 2017 HubSpot Content Trends Survey showed that 53% of people surveyed wanted to see more video content from marketers.[14] The survey also showed that while most people will skim most media, they will thoroughly consume video. Video is one of the most engaging media available—why not leverage that for your practice?

YouTube is owned by Google, and it's a good idea to leverage any Google tool since they are the search giant. In the years to come, we will see how Google and Amazon compete in the digital assistant realm and how it will affect searching.

If you have video available, make sure you put copies of it on a YouTube channel branded with your practice logo, photo, and contact information. Don't forget to let your patients know about your YouTube channel; you can use some of the same ideas mentioned previously in the Instagram section.

Note that video on Facebook should be directly loaded onto that platform, not shared through a YouTube link. A YouTube link will require users to click on it to play your video, whereas videos uploaded directly to Facebook will automatically play for most Facebook and Instagram users, and that's a good thing. Facebook likes to keep users in their walled garden and anything you can do to accommodate patients there, you should. In the case of video on Facebook, allow people to quickly and easily consume the video within Facebook.

Speaking of video on Facebook... You may also want to consider Facebook Live video. Facebook Live is just what it sounds like: live video broadcast on Facebook. The added benefit with live video vs. prerecorded video on Facebook is that Facebook sends out a notification to your Facebook followers that you are live. There are also notifications that shows which of your friends are currently watching Live video. For example, a potential patient may see that her friend is watching your practice's Facebook Live video lunch and learn about teeth whitening. Some teams will do great with live video and others not so much. Know that any video that represents your practice well is good. You can always apply a paid boost to your pre-recorded video to make the most of it.

Online Reviews

Last but certainly not least, know that one of your most powerful marketing tools is review sites. A 2017 BrightLocal Local Consumer Review Survey showed that an incredible 85% of customers trust online reviews as much as they trust a personal recommendation.[15] Every practice needs positive reviews because they are the number-one form of social proof and the number-one way for you to protect your online reputation.

The key to growing positive reviews today is systems. Just like the systems you put in place for many other aspects of your practice that allow you to be successful, having a system in place for your online reviews is crucial. During my live presentations I often ask the audience to participate in discussion about how they are generating reviews. Whether an audience of 30 people or 300, generally about 1/3 of the attendees will say they are asking for reviews all of the time, another 1/3 will say they are asking for reviews some of the time, and the last 1/3 will say they are not asking for reviews at all. Of the people who do not ask for reviews at all, their reasons are that they didn't think to invite reviews, didn't realize how important it is, or they say they don't have time or don't have someone on the team who will handle this.

Which category do you fall into?

- Ask for reviews all the time?

- Ask for reviews some of the time?

- Never ask for reviews?

Below are some of the most popular, effective methods to grow positive reviews for your practice. Every practice can find a method that fits their schedule, budget, and preference—without having to feel desperate or awkward.

One simple method is for your team members or you, the dentist, to invite patients to leave positive reviews whenever they pay you compliments. This might require some role play for you to discover who on your team can best handle this. Discuss all the details with your team, including how exactly you might ask your patient and where in your practice this conversation might take place; e.g., the treatment room, at the front desk when patients are being checked out by the administrative team, etc. For example, you may ask every patient upon completing their appointment:

Admin team member: *How did we do today?*

Patient: *Awesome, I love to get my teeth cleaned by Sara!*

Admin team member: *That's what we love to hear. Thank you for letting me know. I will be sure to let Sara know. :)*

By the way, we have a Facebook page for the practice and I know it would really make Sara's day if you shared your compliment there. (Or state whichever review platform you are trying to grow reviews on.)

Patient: *Of course, I'm happy to.*

During a live event, it's always interesting to see an energetic team member demonstrate for a skeptical team member from a different practice how easily this can be done. It's all about finding the right personality/perspective for the task.

Another system that might be a better fit for your team is to hand out tangibles to encourage patients to leave reviews, like business cards or postcards. Some practices like to hand out these types of materials and have success with it, while others who are paperless don't like the idea of anything printed. If you're reading this and thinking this is too much work, imagine the relief you will have knowing that your reputation will be protected because you have a variety of positive reviews to help shield you.

I also highly recommend that you email patients a survey after their appointments. It's wonderful to see the survey comments and detail that patients will type into their keyboards or devices. Automated email surveys are not only a great way for your practice to be found and to convert new patients, they are also great tools to learn what your patients like most about your practice. I love to see team members get recognized by name in patient reviews. This type of feedback also helps you discover which team members are having the biggest impact with your patients.

Automated surveys are convenient for both you and your patients. They are powerful tools that I think every practice should have in place. Patient engagement systems like Solutionreach™ automatically send surveys to your patients after their appointments. There are many other features and benefits to using patient engagement systems, such as email or text appointment reminders, and you can opt for features such as two-way text communication with patients. For digital-loving patients, two-way text communication is expected, not just a convenience. The Patient-Provider Relationship Study by Solutionreach revealed that 73% of patients (across generations, including Boomers) want the ability to text their doctor.[16]

I have seen automated surveys allow practices to easily and consistently gather hundreds of positive testimonials over the years. These reviews can—and should—be highlighted on your practice website. You can also share copies of reviews to different social media platforms, directly on a Facebook tab (not the News Feed), or share screenshots of reviews to highlight on Instagram.

Another favorite review-boosting technology is BirdEye™. BirdEye is a powerful reputation marketing tool that will make it easy for your patients to review your practice. This technology automatically sends a review request SMS (text) to your patient's cell phone. For patients that prefer text over email, this also ensures your patients will see the review request. With BirdEye, your positive reviews are automatically showcased on your website, Google business profile, Facebook, and Twitter, plus indexed by search engines like Google, Bing, and Yahoo for higher search result ranking. You can also instantly receive review alerts in real-time, so you can quickly and easily address any patient satisfaction issues before they escalate. Visit with Dr. Len Tau at birdeye.com/dental for more information.

There are many different brands, tools, and technologies that you can implement to grow your reviews. The key is to find a trusted and proven process or technology, like those mentioned here, that works for you and stick with it. Review generating systems are an absolute must-have for every practice. Remember that <u>positive online reviews are the number-one way for you to protect your online reputation</u>. If you ever have a grumpy patient that leaves one negative comment, your dozens of positive comments will help to minimize or drown it out. Most importantly, positive online reviews are a powerful marketing tool. Reviews provide the social proof that patients want to see before they feel comfortable enough becoming a new patient, accepting treatment, or referring to your practice.

So where should you spend your social media time and resources? The most important question is, **"Where do your ideal patients spend *their* time?"**

In the next chapter we'll explore what patients like to see once they find you.

Getting Liked

Now that you've been found online, how do you get patients to like you? And why would you want patients to like you—does it really matter? Some people might say having likes on your Facebook page, followers on Instagram, or connections on LinkedIn are nothing more than ego-builders or vanity data. In reality, quality likes or follows on your business page or Instagram are valuable because these are either actual patients of yours, people who are interested in becoming patients, or supporters of your practice. Quality followers are people who have decided they not only like you but want to subscribe to updates from you. By liking, following, or connecting with you on social media, those patients are agreeing to keep your name and face in front of them on a consistent basis. How awesome is that?

For social media-savvy patients, seeing a practice with a healthy number of likes (this number is different for every practice, but let's say 200 as a general number) and an active, engaged community that likes and comments on your posts and updates, provides social proof that you might be as awesome as you said you were on your website. Social proof/being liked is an invaluable puzzle piece in the patient conversion process. Think back to the studies I mentioned that showed the extensive research people typically do when vetting dentists or specialists, including:

- Visiting website
- Reading online reviews
- Watching video
- Checking social networks

Without social proof, you have a roadblock in patient conversion. <u>The most dangerous and vulnerable place to be today is anonymous</u>. In our busy society, armed with smartphones that can research anything, anytime, anywhere, people do not want to guess what they can expect when they choose your practice. They want to know as much as possible, and part of reassuring people considering becoming a patient is showing how well-liked you are.

Make a Good First Impression

One of the first steps to being liked on social media is to make a good first impression. Put your best foot forward. Allow patients who already know you to easily recognize your practice social media by including your logo and photos of your team as well as the interior and exterior of your practice. If your website's theme and branding colors are primarily blue and grey, make sure you also include blue and grey in your custom graphics or include a similar color scheme. This attention to detail will make for a congruent experience for both current and potential new patients.

You may have heard the phrase "you never get a second chance to make a first impression." A large part of making a good impression on social media is to be **authentic**. Because photos are often a catalyst for emotional connection on social media, make sure you have plenty of photos of you and your team in cover photos, profiles, or posts—not stock photos, but photos of real people. When people land on your practice social media, you have seconds to capture their attention and draw them in (remember, humans' attention spans are now shorter than that of a goldfish!), and chances are better you will accomplish this with pictures of real people.

This doesn't mean you can't ever use stock photography; there is still a limited place for that. However, the majority of photos should be of your practice and team, and ideally, they should be current photos, unless you are posting a "Throwback Thursday" or "Way Back Wednesday" post. Remember, the best and most effective social media is rooted in authenticity.

This is where people often begin to ask, "What should we post on our social media?" The answer is to let your values guide you. Think about what is most important for you to convey about your brand. What is it that you want people to perceive or think of when they find your practice online? The marketing term for this is brand perception.

Do you want them to think you have a practice focused on excellence, technology, and philanthropy? Maybe you're a pediatric practice, and you want patients to think your practice is friendly, fun, and family-oriented. Perhaps your practice is focused on seeing adults for smile makeovers or for treatments related to overall health; then you'd have a completely different set of objectives.

One of my biggest pet peeves is seeing a practice website that is meticulous and represents a luxury brand, only to visit their social media and find it looks nothing like their website brand, with blurry images or tacky comics. *insert face palm here*

Consider and choose three different adjectives to describe your ideal practice brand. These adjectives should reflect values that are important to you (the dentist or specialist owner) and reflect what you want people to perceive when they see you and your practice online. Don't worry, everyone has a brand, it's just that some people may not recognize it yet. If you think about it, we all have a set of values that drive our personal brands. For doctors, your personal brands will often be similar in your business. If you are someone who appreciates fitness or luxury or environmental awareness personally, chances are you aren't going to turn that part of your life off when you step into your practice.

See the sampling of adjectives below. Do you see some words that resonate with you? Feel free to pick your own adjectives that best describe your current practice or the ideal practice you are striving for. There are unlimited adjectives to choose from! Here are just a few:

Family	Personal Growth
Fun	Environmental Awareness
Luxury	Adventure
Community	Fitness
Philanthropy	Friendliness
Excellence	Education
Whole Body Health	Sophistication

This is an exercise anyone with a social media presence should do. The exercise is best done by the doctor/owner and then communicated to the social media manager, and from there to the entire team. These adjectives will serve as a guide to help your social media manager determine what the best type of content, images, video, etc. are to share. If the doctor has not communicated this to the team, then the social media manager is stuck trying to guess what your practice wants to communicate.

If you already know what you want your social media presence to say about you and your practice, congratulations! This information will not only help you decide what type of content to share, it guides you authentically. Some doctors or office managers have "a-ha" moments upon doing this exercise. One doctor shared that he thought his social media content was "off" but he couldn't define exactly why. Once he did the exercise and discovered his adjectives, he realized there were many posts and images that he described as "tacky" on his social media and he wanted to shift towards a more sophisticated brand to match his meticulous dentistry.

Choose Your Brand Adjectives

- Take a few minutes alone to sit and think

- Take a few deep breaths; close your eyes if you like

- What three adjectives come to mind when you think of your existing or ideal practice? (remember there are a multitude of adjectives you can choose from)

- Think about what is important to you personally if that's helpful

- Don't spend too much time overthinking it... Often your gut will prompt you within a few minutes and if you overthink this, your brain will interrupt your intuition.

For the more private doctors out there, understand that we are aiming towards being personable - I'm not recommending you share anything that you consider private. There are ways to share content in alignment with your brand and share some personality without making you uncomfortable. I worked with a doctor a few years ago who said he didn't want to have his picture on social media. He simply wasn't comfortable with it. We talked about what he enjoyed doing outside of the practice, and he said, "I love to cycle. That's what I do when I'm not in the practice."

I told him to take some pictures of the landscapes where he cycled. He happened to live in a beautiful area of the country, so he provided us with pictures of the ocean, the boardwalk, and the mountains. He didn't have to be on social media personally, but we were still able to share something that gave his patients something to talk about and connect with on a human level— while also sharing his overall passion for fitness.

Another dentist we worked with told us the same thing. She didn't want to be the "focus of social media." It just wasn't something she was comfortable with. When we talked about what she enjoyed outside of the practice, she told me she had a passion for gardening. She also had a labradoodle dog that happened to be adorable and very photogenic. She provided some photos of her garden and her dog, and patients were able to see a glimpse of her human side without having to share anything uncomfortable for the dentist.

Think about the things you enjoy outside of the office. It might be gardening, hiking, or volunteering at the local humane society in your free time. These hobbies or interests could all lead to different types of excellent social posts.

One of the most popular posts we have shared for practices is a "get to know your dentist or specialist" post, such as:

Dr. Smith loves getting to know her patients! So we thought you might like to know a little more about her, too.

Favorite type of music: 80's hits.

Favorite dessert: Homemade chocolate chip cookies.

Favorite hobby: Hiking.

Favorite sports team: Her son's local hockey team, the Flying Penguins.

Favorite animal: Her cat, Ginger.

In this case, we'd post the above information with a photo of the doctor and her son in his hockey gear, or with her cat, Ginger. Patients love seeing this. Here are the benefits to this type of post:

- It humanizes the doctor
- It gives patients something to chitchat about with the doctor/team at their appointments

- It allows patients to discover common interests
- It often makes your patients smile :)
- Most importantly, this type of sharing and authenticity helps grow trust and relationships.

If you want to personalize posts that highlight others, you can feature team members—and you can do this in many different ways. Aside from showing photos of your team in your office, consider this: one of our clients' team members shared photos of her adorable goats (yes, goats) and the patients commented and liked this more than any other post we'd ever shared for the practice. You may not have a team member with cute goats, but there are many brilliant, fun, and wonderful people in our industry who wouldn't mind sharing their own special tidbit.

You can also look outside of your practice. For example, give kudos to a local business. Maybe you get sandwiches or pizza from the same place for your staff meetings every month. Give a shout-out to the deli or pizza place owner, tag their page, and give them a virtual pat on the back.

Many of our clients support non-profits by donating or volunteering, and those topics are a great way to both generate good will and share with patients and the community what your practice stands for.

For example:
- Veterans Groups
- Make-a-Wish Foundation
- Humane Society
- Boys and Girls Clubs of America
- Oral Cancer Cause
- Toys for Tots

Perfection Paralysis

A wise coach once told me, **"perfection stands in the way of progress."** I see many dentists who won't update their photo because they don't have a perfect replacement. It used to be that professional, perfectly-staged photos were the only photos that were acceptable for website bios or brochures, and while those photos are still great, today being real is often winning over being perfect.

Dentistry is a profession filled with meticulous personalities. People who like more detail than not, fine lines drawn between black and white, and margins measuring up just so. And that's great, right? We want our dentists and surgeons to be precision-minded when it comes to our health. Likewise, we want practice administrators and insurance coordinators to be detail-oriented as they orchestrate teams and manage our financial statements.

So, naturally, when social media emerged in dentistry, the field welcomed rules of engagement. Articles and advice about etiquette and how to do social media *right* became popular. I authored some of those early lessons, preaching about what you should and shouldn't do with your practice social media accounts, and sometimes personal profiles as well.

The tides began to turn sometime between 2007, when Facebook business pages launched, and today, and **being real is now winning over being perfect**. Of course there are still many practices and dental professionals that have impeccable brands, picture-perfect photos, and stellar videos. But what's most important is that your content reflects your individual practice values, brand, and personality. (Remember your three adjectives from the earlier exercise to help you to determine how you want your brand to be perceived.)

I think the desire for real versus perfect is largely a result of the growing population of smartphones. Consider those devices that are used less for calls and more for texting and photos. Our beloved devices never leave our sides and allow us to research anything, anytime, anywhere. Most who own smartphones have learned to cut through the facade of websites and reference social media or review sites to learn the social truth, the real truth. Smartphones have likely played a large part in our curiosity and appetite for raw truth today.

Your Vibe Attracts Your Tribe

The phrases "like attracts like" and "your vibe attracts your tribe" have never been more relevant. It won't take long for you to find people you are drawn to when everyone is being more real than perfect. Some of us may have a harder time peeling back the layers of what we are comfortable showing—and not—in our public persona. Be patient with yourself, and at the same time, be aware of perfection paralysis.

Honor Patients' News Feeds

In dentistry, we walk a fine line of not overstepping our welcome in people's news feeds. Unlike brands whose content is filled with puppies, cupcakes, or cute videos, in the dental profession we have to be conscientious about how often we post and what we post. One of my pet peeves is hearing consultants recommend posting multiple times per day and having X number of posts minimum per week. I say, post when you have something good to share. We will discuss planning content later in the book, but if you are spending copious amounts of time trying to come up with content to meet quantity criteria, you are likely compromising quality. You can rely on boosts and paid promotions to help you expand your visibility for your good content. **Focus on quality over quantity, always.** This has been our mantra over the years and it continues to serve us and our clients well.

Once people find you on social media, they should see a combination of social and dental/clinical information, such as 80% social and 20% dental or clinical content. Eighty-percent social scares some dentists and office managers, or whoever is in charge of social media, because they don't always know how to find enough social content for the practice.

Here is a list of questions you can use to brainstorm with your team and generate post ideas for your practice. Set aside 15 minutes at your next team meeting to discuss:

- What hobbies does the doctor or team enjoy?

- What do you do when you aren't in the office?

- What do you love about living in your city or neighborhood?

- What special activities or events are coming up in your office or community?

- Do you have any birthdays, anniversaries, or special dates to celebrate?

- Are any of your team members willing to be featured with a fun photo and snippet about what they love most about what they do?

- Do you donate or volunteer for any non-profits, missions, or organizations?

- Do you have any seasonal reminders to share? For example: wisdom tooth removal during school breaks, insurance expiring/renewing, special holiday hours, etc.

- Are you a fan of any local businesses that you can give a "shout out" to?

You may also want to buy the book *365 Days of Social Posts for Dentistry,* which is a handy resource filled with post ideas. You can find it on Amazon or at www.rachelmele.com/book-2/ and let the author, Rachel Mele, know that Rita sent you.

On the opposite side of the spectrum, sometimes dentists and teams forget it's important to share dental or clinical content. You may not get 100 likes on your post about dental implants without applying some advertising budget to it, but it's still important for patients scrolling through social media to see the types of procedures you want to do more of.

Think about it. What procedures are you most interested in growing in your practice? What treatments do you most enjoy providing?

Most dentists can answer that question right away. Take a look at your social media platforms and make sure patients can see those types of procedures on your social media. In many cases, they cannot. I think that's because social media experts have reinforced how important it is to be social on social media. And yes, that is important, however, you need to balance out both social and dental (or whatever your specialty is) if you want to attract your ideal patients AND do more of the treatments that you most enjoy. Putting a content strategy in place that is in alignment with your goals is the only way to be intentional about growing a practice that you love.

Now that you're found and liked, let's talk about getting patients.

Getting Patients

I hope you are beginning to see from the research and examples I've provided that social media has become a critical piece in your overall online presence puzzle. Without it, you are either anonymous or potentially lacking the detail that patients need to see in order to feel comfortable becoming a patient or accepting treatment from you. **Social media is no longer a "nice to have"- it's a "must-have."**

After you've grown your visibility, shared some of your human side along with a bit of clinical information, and attracted patients' attention, how do you acquire patients over time with social media? It comes down to strategy and systems.

If you aren't active on social media, you probably don't realize that patients are asking questions through social media, Facebook, or Instagram. It's a convenient place for them to type a question out to you because they are already spending so much time there. You have to think of social media not as just a marketing tool or a short-term tactic, but as a long-term communication tool. Once you've made that shift in your mind, you can begin to see how important systems and strategy are when it comes to acquiring patients via social media.

Strategy and Systems

Just like the systems you have in place in other aspects of your practice, you must have a strategy and system for social media to be efficient, effective, and successful long-term.

The strategy of social media for your practice includes the components we've reviewed in previous sections of this book, getting found and getting liked. In order to implement your strategy, you need systems to launch and maintain your efforts over time.

While some practices have been successful doing social media off the cuff, **the only way to be strategic is through planning**. I'm happy to share our proven One Page Social Media Marketing Plan with you. The questions in the plan are the same questions we've answered for ourselves and our clients to help grow our business and our clients' practices over the years. Your plan answers will help you determine whether or not you can actually implement a social media strategy yourself and maintain it over time.

You can access the One Page Social Media Plan at **www.RitaZamora.com/SpecialBookBonus**. Also included in your special bonus downloads is a sample Social Media for Dentistry Job Description. (You're welcome!)

To manage social media long-term, you need to have some key systems in place, and that includes having someone to manage your social media. It may be someone internal or it may be an external vendor. It used to be that social media could only be properly handled internally, but today there are some practices that have become overwhelmed by the different tools and options and the time social media can take to manage. In some cases, the multitudes of advertising options and complexities have put teams over the top, so they decide to work with someone externally.

Who's going to manage social media for you? Will it be done internally or externally? These are some of the questions in your social media plan you will need to consider.

What are you going to share or post on a consistent basis? Having an editorial calendar in place is an essential time-saver, and it's the only way for you to be strategic with social media. Often, practices share content, photos, and videos spontaneously. They may be having fun in the moment, which is great, but strategy is often left out. With an editorial calendar, you decide what you want to make sure you promote this month, the following month, six months from now and possibly next year. At minimum, you should plan for the month ahead.

The mention of an editorial calendar is enough to stumble some team members. Your editorial calendar can be as simple as using a scheduling tool. Facebook has a free scheduling tool you can use to create draft ideas, make revisions, and schedule your posts and boosts for the future. You can find the Facebook scheduling tool on your Facebook Business page. If you are posting to multiple social media platforms, you should use a tool like Hootsuite™, a social media management program that will allow you to plan, create, and schedule for multiple platforms, including Facebook, Instagram, LinkedIn, Twitter, etc.

Some practices post a giant sticky note in their break room where they can brainstorm and collaborate on future content ideas. Whether you prefer paper or digital planning, it's important for you to document and plan what you want to achieve, otherwise you will be back to spontaneity which takes your eyes off the goal. Spontaneity can also be more time-consuming and stressful for some team members if they feel they have to constantly come up with ideas.

What Type of Practice Do You Want To Grow?

When creating your editorial calendar and planning your content, think about what is most important for you to promote. You can answer that question by determining what type of practice you're looking to grow and what types of procedures you want to do more of.

Remember, social media has become a pay-to-play world and you need to have a budget to fully leverage it. Of all the tactics mentioned, the key to continually growing your visibility and results are Facebook boosts and/or Instagram ads.

Don't forget to download my 5 X 5 Boost Formula at **www.RitaZamora.com/SpecialBookBonus** to learn how to best boost your Facebook posts.

As you are creating your future editorial calendar, plan and note what you want to promote throughout the month. If you want to grow your teeth whitening services or dental implants, or maybe it's nearing wisdom tooth removal season, you'll want to include those topics in your editorial plan and note your need for boosts/ads accordingly.

Or maybe you're planning for a special event. Perhaps you are donating a day of dentistry for veterans, holding a food drive or coat drive, or launching a fun contest or giveaway to generate goodwill and spread the word about your practice.

Whatever your events or promotions are, you want to include them in your editorial calendar well in advance. This will give you adequate time for promotion, and since you're going to spend money on sponsored posts for these events, you'll want to plan for that in advance too. Once you have your editorial calendar planned out, you can have fun and be spontaneous with other content. You will rest assured that you have all the important, strategic business-building content ready to go, and any additional content you post will just enhance the plan you have in place.

Tracking

One common question some practices struggle to answer is how to determine where patients are finding them online. Remember that research shows patients are visiting a variety of online touchpoints—not just one site. Don't make the mistake of thinking only one site is delivering all your patients. Think of your online presence like a puzzle, with many puzzle pieces that need to be in place; for example:

- Your website

- Google My Business listing

- Online reviews

- Social media

- SEO (search engine optimization), online listings optimized, etc.

Just as you have a system in place for your social media strategy, you should make sure you have a system or systems in place for tracking how new patients found you. There are various methods you can use to determine where patients found you.

Let's start with your intake forms. Whether you're using paper forms or you've gone digital, many intake forms ask, "Who may we thank for referring you?" While this question is still important, you should also provide the opportunity for patients to share how they may have researched you.

Typically patients might say, "My friend, Susan, referred me," and practices will just run with that and say, "We need to thank Susan for referring her friend." This is great, and I agree that we need to pay attention to referrals. However, we should not leave the referral source at that. Instead, your intake form should also include the question, "How did you find us?" Especially with digital forms, patients will take the time to share more detail with you.

You can include checkboxes to allow patients to share all the places where they may have seen you online. For example:

Have you seen us on:

☐ Facebook

☐ Instagram

☐ Google Reviews

☐ YouTube video, etc., etc.

Remember to put checkboxes next to these options so patients can easily click them when completing their intake questionnaires. This gives patients an opportunity to share exactly how they found you and/or where they may have researched you or ran across your name. Collecting this data also gives you an opportunity to understand how valuable your investments in social media are.

Another option you may consider implementing is LocalMed™ technology. LocalMed is a real-time online scheduling tool. What I love about LocalMed is that adding their scheduling link to your website, Facebook business page, Instagram page, or Google My Business profile allows patients to book appointments directly from those pages, plus the technology tracks where the appointment scheduling was initiated. It's a win-win when you are providing a convenient service for patients that also allows you to track exactly where they scheduled their appointments.

The segment of patients who don't want to talk to another human to schedule an appointment and just want to book online will continue to grow. Don't forget the busy mom who wants to book an appointment with you, but the only time she has free is at 9 p.m. after she put the kids to bed and now your office is closed. LocalMed is currently the only real-time online scheduling tool, so check them out.

Some teams opt to go through a lengthy interview process with patients to discover exactly how they heard of the practice and what their online experience was. After they've welcomed the patient to the practice and the patient has had a great experience with them, the dentist or a team member may ask, "How did you find us exactly?" If the patient says, "I Googled you," they ask more in-depth questions and document the patient's feedback.

For specialists, I recommend paying particular attention to these tracking options. Often teams will automatically put the patient's general dentist in the database as the referral source. This is problematic because your reports will indicate you are getting referrals from someone when there's a possibility the patient found you online and chose you themselves.

Which tracking methods do you have in place? Are you using a combination of systems to track?

Remember, systems and strategies are the keys to success in your practice and the same applies to your social media marketing.

Final Thoughts

Over the years, I've observed social media marketing agencies come and go. In some cases, they were failed attempts at heavily leveraging generic content on behalf of their dentist clients. I never liked the generic content model, mainly because I thought many of the topics were uninteresting to patients, but most importantly, because I felt they cheated dentists and specialists out of showing their authentic selves (which is what patients really want to see and what gets the best results).

Below are several examples of generic posts that I recently found on one dentist's page:

- Fun Fact! Floss was first manufactured in 1896 and was made of silk.

- How well do you know your dental facts? Click here to learn more.

- Want to know how to harden your tooth enamel?

What is even sadder to see is when these generic topics are posted on behalf of specialists, which make the posts even less effective as they often aren't even relevant.

Over the years we've monitored and compared the data between generic posts and authentic/personalized posts. The engagement received for generic posts is often poor— engagement being clicks, likes, or comments. In the case of a practice with a few hundred Facebook page likes, the posts listed above resulted in zero post likes and reached an average of 6-9 people each. Compare those stats for the same page who posted a photo of their donation efforts for an event in their community and that post received 14 likes and reached 126 people. That is over 1,000% better reach and visibility, not to mention engagement, for the practice from the authentic post vs. the generic post. It's a 1,000% better opportunity for your practice to be in front of potential and existing patients' eyes. This conservative case is just one example of what we see every day. **Authenticity rules.**

In this book, you have the guidelines to follow for how to get found on social media. <u>Once you are found, patients want to see YOU, your team, and what's unique and special about your practice</u>.

Share content that appeals to your ideal patient. Think about what procedures you want to be known for… What is special about you, your team, and your practice? Share photos and video of you and your team—or the things you love about your practice, your community, or the world. Share about anything connected to you, so you don't have to rely on generic messaging.

You have all that it takes to be awesome on social media. Be yourself, share your light and personality, have fun if you like. There are many dentists and specialists who are already out there sharing their awesomeness every day. If you need inspiration, follow some dental superstars on Facebook or Instagram and see for yourself.

Every dentist, specialist, and team is unique and I believe you all have something special to offer. I am confident you can make the most of your social media to **get found, get liked, and get patients**. I look forward to hearing from you and seeing you in the social media sphere soon. Cheers!

Next Steps to Get Found, Get Liked, and Get Patients

I hope you found some motivation, tips, and answers for either getting started with social media or taking your social media efforts to a whole new level. You may have found relief in the validation that what you're already doing is exactly what you need to be doing. If you've felt enlightened, validated, or motivated by what you've read, and you're ready to jump in and get started, great! Here are some potential next steps you can take right away:

For those of you just getting started

1. Create your Facebook Business Page

2. Get new team photos

3. Invite your team and local friends and family to like your page and share your page with their local network

For those of you taking things to the next level

1. Set a goal to grow more online reviews

2. Place 1-3 Facebook boosts/ads consistently, every month

3. Create more video, perhaps Facebook or Instagram Live video, or take your Instagram Stories to the next level

Remember to take advantage of all my bonus downloads for this book, available at **www.RitaZamora.com/SpecialBookBonus**:

1. My One Page Social Media Plan
2. My sample Social Media for Dentistry Job Description
3. My 5 X 5 Boost Formula to show you step by step how to best boost your Facebook posts

Start by completing the One Page Social Media Plan. This will help you determine how likely you are to successfully manage social media internally. If you fill out the One Page Social Media Plan and feel confident that you're already handling and managing the tasks involved very well, then you're well on your way to social media success. Congratulations!

If you're excited and motivated, but still feel like you need help, don't worry! You have options.

While I have a Bachelor's degree in Business and Marketing, there are no formal degrees that I'm aware of in Facebook, Instagram, or Snapchat. You can self-teach. That's exactly what I've done over the years. Since 2007, when Facebook first released Facebook Business pages, we've been helping practices with social media. I'm a self-taught social media professional, and you could be, too, if you have the time, effort, and energy to do so.

Of course, there's an abundance of free information online. Just be careful you don't get yourself into an endless rabbit hole. Know that there are people out there who can help save you a lot of time and make it simpler to achieve your social media goals of getting found, getting liked, and getting patients.

On the other hand, if you've completed the One Page Social Media Marketing Plan and you feel like there are some things in the plan that you can't be held accountable for or you struggle to understand, or you don't know exactly what the next steps are, or if you don't have the time, effort, or energy to manage this... then it's time to hire some help. Hopefully, that will be us. We look forward to hearing from you!

If you'd like us to help, go to **www.RitaZamora.com**, or reach out to me at Rita@RitaZamora.com, and we can get started with your social media success strategy today.

How We Can Help You

You're ready to get started with social media, or maybe you want to take your social media to the next level. But you're not exactly sure what to do, or you're not sure what's effective, or you just don't have the interest or the time.

That's where Rita Zamora Connections comes in. We help dentists and specialists just like you every day.

We're here to help at any level. Whether it's hourly assistance or full-service support, we have you and your team covered.

We offer one-on-one virtual training by the hour, tailored to the exact issues you need help with.

We also offer monthly support with fully customized social media services, including social media ad placement, monitoring and managing. We'll handle everything from A to Z for you.

How It Works

Step 1: We schedule a strategy session with you and talk about your goals, the type of patient that you want to attract, and the type of procedures that you want to grow more of in your practice.

Step 2: We work with you to craft a social media strategy for you that you can begin to implement right away.

Step 3: We provide you with the information that you need to run with in your practice if you're managing your social media yourself. If you prefer, we handle everything for you and your team can focus on what they do best—which is provide the best dental care possible.

Many practices are not fully leveraging social media and they're missing out on visibility, a strong online reputation, word of mouth, and new patients.

Now you can Get Found, Get Liked, and Get Patients and it's easier than you think.

If you'd like our help, send an email to **Rita@RitaZamora.com** and we'll take it from there.

Acknowledgements

Thank you to my husband, Michael McClure, for always believing in me and for your love and encouragement. Many thanks to my talented team member and meticulous editor, Laura Mallas, for making me look good in print and digital. I would not be in the profession I am in today if it weren't for the dental family I worked with for many years. Thank you, Dr. Marc Reissner, for your leadership, mentorship, and for creating valuable opportunities for your team to learn, grow, and thrive. Thank you, Dr. Neil Neugeboren, for your kindness, leadership, and passion for the profession. Thank you, Dr. Alan Pomeranz, for your leadership, flair, and for making the workplace fun. Luci Berardi, thank you, for being a dear and incredible best friend, co-creator, and Practice Administrator extraordinaire. To all of my team members, current and past, I am grateful and blessed to work alongside you, or to have worked with you; thank you. And of course, special thanks to all of our wonderful clients who entrust us with their social media and practice reputation—I sincerely appreciate you.

About the Author

Rita Zamora is a highly sought-after international speaker and published author on social media and online reputation management. Her advice on managing your online reputation was published in the American Dental Association's Practical Guide to Expert Business Strategies and she served as a Contributing Faculty Member on the topic of marketing for the 2015 American Dental Association's Center for Success Certificate Program.

Rita is the founder of Rita Zamora Connections, an established dental consulting firm that specializes in social media marketing for dentists and specialists. Their agency provides highly customized solutions and encourages genuine personal interaction between their dentist and specialist clients and their patients. Since 2008, they've worked with hundreds of dental professionals, through speaking engagements and their agency, to train or assist them in authentic and valuable online interactions.

Rita graduated magna cum laude from the University of Colorado with a bachelor's degree in business and marketing and has over 20 years of experience working in the business of dentistry. When she is not working, Rita enjoys unplugging in nature and hiking with her husband, Michael, and their dog, Winnifred, in beautiful Colorado.

"No matter who you are or what kind of company or organization you work for, your number-one job is to tell your story to the consumer wherever they are, and preferably at the moment they are deciding to make a purchase."

— Gary Vaynerchuk, Author of *Jab, Jab, Jab, Right Hook: How to Tell Your Story in a Noisy Social World*

Industry-Specific Resources Mentioned in this Book

In this book, I mention by name many products and services that you may find helpful. On occasion I have been sponsored by some of these companies, and I have an affiliate relationship with others. However, I only endorse products I truly consider valuable to clients, and I only recommend a product to an individual practice if I believe that is in the best interest of meeting that practice's particular needs. I encourage you to research all your options and select the best fit for your practice.

Patient Financing

CareCredit (ask your local representative about the Path to Purchase study): carecredit.com

Patient Engagement System

Solutionreach: solutionreach.com

Online Reviews, Reputation Marketing

BirdEye (ask for Dr. Len Tau): birdeye.com/dental

Real-Time, Online Scheduling Technology

LocalMed: localmed.com

If you're looking for recommendations on a product or service not listed above, we are happy to help! Just contact us at **ritazamora.com** and ask.

Endnotes

[1] "Mobile Fact Sheet," Pew Research Center, Feb. 5, 2018, http://www.pewinternet.org/fact-sheet/mobile/

[2] "Zero Moment of Truth (ZMOT)," Google, 2011-2014, https://www.thinkwithgoogle.com/marketing-resources/micro-moments/zero-moment-truth/

[3] "A Field Guide to the US Digital Travel Booking Journey," FacebookIQ, Sept. 2016, https://fbinsights.files.wordpress.com/2016/09/facebooki q_mobilecompassfieldguide.pdf ; Facebook-commissioned survey of 2,400 people in the U.S. aged 18–64 who had booked a business or leisure trip in the previous three months, Nov 2015–May 2016.

[4] "Consumers' Path To Healthcare Purchases Study" (white paper), Path to Purchases Research conducted for CareCredit by Rothstein Tauber Inc., 2014. https://www.carecredit.com/assets/views/news/files/139 48_Whitepaper_072315.pdf

[5] "Consumers Path to Healthcare Purchases Study" (article), CareCredit, July 22, 2015, https://www.carecredit.com/newsroom/consumers-path-to-healthcare/

[6] Marikar, Sheila, "How ColourPop Is Putting A New Face On The Online Cosmetics Business," Fast Company, Apr. 17, 2017, https://www.fastcompany.com/40400780/how-colourpop-is-putting-a-new-face-on-the-online-cosmetics-business

[7] Dsouza, Karina and Sarkar, Indranil, "Coty's recent acquisitions fuel quarterly profit, revenue beat," Reuters, Feb. 8, 2018, https://www.nasdaq.com/article/cotys-

recent-acquisitions-fuel-quarterly-profit-revenue-beat-20180208-00850

[8] "Shades for success: Influence in the beauty market," Deloitte, 2017, https://www2.deloitte.com/content/dam/Deloitte/cn/Documents/international-business-support/deloitte-cn-ibs-france-beauty-market-en-2017.pdf

[9] Hanauer, Zheng, Singer, Gebremariam, and Davis, "Public Awareness, Perception, and Use of Online Physician Rating Sites," Journal of the American Medical Association, Feb. 19, 2014, https://jamanetwork.com/journals/jama/fullarticle/1829975

[10] "Social Media Fact Sheet," Pew Research Center, Feb. 5, 2018, http://www.pewinternet.org/fact-sheet/social-media/

[11] Boland, Brian, "Organic Reach on Facebook: Your Questions Answered," Facebook, June 2014, https://www.facebook.com/business/news/Organic-Reach-on-Facebook

[12] Castillo, Michelle, "Instagram reaches 700 million users at its fastest-ever growth rate," CNBC, Apr. 26, 2017, ww.cnbc.com/2017/04/26/instagram-has-700-million-users.html

[13] "Attention Span Statistics," Statistic Brain, July 2, 2016, https://www.statisticbrain.com/attention-span-statistics/

[14] An, Mimi, "Content Trends: Preferences Emerge Along Generational Fault Lines," HubSpot Research, Nov. 6, 2017, https://research.hubspot.com/content-trends-preferences

[15] "Local Consumer Review Survey," BrightLocal, 2017, https://www.brightlocal.com/learn/local-consumer-review-survey/

[16] "The Patient-Provider Relationship Study," Solutionreach, https://www.solutionreach.com/patient-provider-relationship-study

Made in the USA
Middletown, DE
01 December 2018